I'm on the naughty list.
Santa checked it twice.

Santa Claus has the right idea. **Visit people only once a year.**

Christmas cookies are the only reason to bake.

I told my family I wanted to stop exchanging gifts, but **they just gave me the gift of disapproval.**

I wouldn't say Santa was lazy, but **he only works one day a year.**

Why did Santa's helper see the doctor?

He had a severe case of tinselitis.

The early present is worth two under the tree.

Christmas is the season when you light up your house and darken your wallet.

I'd tell you a Christmas tree joke, but it's really sappy.

Santa’s favorite place to deliver gifts?
Idaho – he can ho, ho, ho while he's there.

Elves are always calm because they know the ins and outs of elf-control.

Christmas is Claus for celebration!

Christmas Dad Jokes

How do snowmen greet each other?

"Ice to meet you!"

What did the beaver say to the Christmas tree?

"Nice gnawing you!"

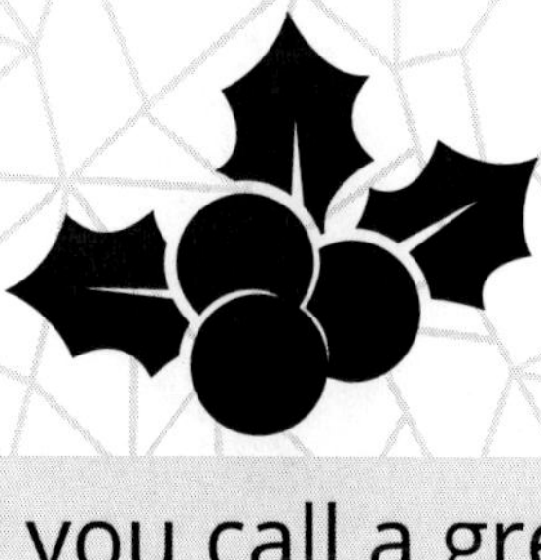

What do you call a greedy elf?

Elfish.

What do you call a reindeer that tells jokes?

Comed-deer.

What do sheep say to each other at Christmastime?

Merry Christmas to ewe!

Why did Rudolph apply for a job?

He was tired of being un-employ-deer.

Why did the Christmas tree go to the barber?
Because it needed a trim!

What do you get if you cross a snowman and a vampire?
Frostbite!

Why was the math book sad at Christmas? **Because it had too many problems.**

How does a snowman get around?

By riding an "icicle"!

What do you call a cat on the beach during Christmas time?

Sandy Claws!

Why did the gingerbread man go to the doctor?

Because he was feeling crumby!

What do you call a snowman party? **A snowball!**

Why was the Christmas tree so bad at sewing? **Because it kept dropping its needles!**

Why did Santa go to music school? **To improve his "wrap" skills!**

What do you call an elf who sings?

A wrapper!

What's a snowman's favorite cereal?

Frosted Flakes!

What do you call a snowman with a lot of money?

Frosty the Snowbank!

Why was the snowman looking through the carrots?

He was picking his nose!

What do you get if you cross a Christmas tree with an iPad?

A pineapple!

What did the gingerbread cookie use to fix his house?

Icing and gumdrops!

What's Santa's favorite pizza?

One that's deep-pan, crisp, and even!

What goes 'oh oh oh!'?

Santa walking backwards.

What do you get if you cross Santa with a duck?

A Christmas quacker!

Christmas Knock, knock.

Knock, knock.
Who's there?
Candle.
Candle who?
Candle be the light of your holiday!

Knock, knock.
Who's there?
Wrap.
Wrap who?
Wrap all your presents yet?

Christmas Knock, knock.

Knock, knock.
Who's there?
Snow.
Snow who?
Snow use – I've forgotten my name again!

Knock, knock.
Who's there?
Yule.
Yule who?
Yule know it's Christmas when your tree is up!

Jokes on Fatherhood and Fatherly Advice

When does a joke become
a "dad joke?"
When it becomes apparent!

If you ever get cold,
just stand in a corner.
They're usually 90 degrees.

Why did the man call the police
when my son wouldn't nap?
He was resisting a rest.

What does Batman do
for Father's Day?
Nothing.

Did you hear about the little boy
who was named after his father ?
They called him Dad!

What do you call
a multiple choice dad joke?
A pop quiz.

What did the German brat say to his father?

You're the wurst!

What did the bicycle call its dad?

Pop-cycle.

My son and I don't always see eye to eye because we both wear glasses.

Knock Knock
Who's there?
Rio!
Rio who?
Rio-rrange your bedroom please!

Knock Knock
Who's there!
Olive!
Olive who?
Olive you too, honeybunch!

My son and I don't always see eye to eye because we both wear glasses.

Always remember these 2 words in your life and many doors will open for you: **push and pull.**

Jokes About School and Knowledge

Did you hear about the kidnapping at school?
It's fine, he woke up.

15+15 is thirty.
16+16 is thirty **too**.

What do I owe ya?
asks the neutron.
"For you No charge."

Hey Math – grow up and solve your own problems.

Did you hear about the book on anti-gravity?
It was impossible to put down.

I was writing a paper on my grandfather...
But had to stop because he was moving so much.

Knock Knock
Who's there!
Abe!
Abe who?
Abe C D E F G H...!

What is the frat guy's favorite ion?
Bromide.

I was going to say a chemistry joke. But I was afraid I wouldn't get a reaction.

I came up with a hilarious joke about format but the margin was too small to contain it.

What kind of stretches does a pencil do?
Ticonder-Yoga.

I wish I had a more acidic wit. Unfortunately mine's very basic.

Why doesn't communism work in a school environment? Because everyone would get the same Marx.

There are 10 types of people in the world: Those that can count and those that can't.

Study what you love and you'll never work a day in your life. Because nobody is hiring in your field.

Authorized,
Bona Fide,
Established...
those are some
Legit synonyms.

What did the band director say
to the misbehaving kid?
You're in treble mister!

I estimate 70% of my work
conversations are just me
quoting made up statistics.

Why did the chicken cross the Mobius Strip?

To get to the same side.

Why do chemists enjoy working with ammonia?

Because it's pretty basic stuff.

Holiday Jokes

What did Adam say to
Eve on Christmas?
It's Christmas Eve.

What did the beaver say
to the Christmas tree?
It was nice gnawing you.

What's the best country to go
to for Thanksgiving?
Turkey.

What is the best Christmas gift?
A broken drum.
It can't be beaten.

What does Santa love to
eat for breakfast?
Frosted Flakes.

How did Santa ask
Rudolph about the
weather?
He asked, **"Do you think**
it will rain, dear?"

What other name can you call Santa's little helpers?
The subordinate Clauses.

What is the most popular music in the North Pole?
It's w**rap**.

What is a dog's favorite Christmas song
Fleas Navidad.

What is Santa's tax status?

Elf-employed.

Knock Knock

Who's there!

Simmy!

Simmy who?

Simmy a Christmas card!

Did you hear about the man who stole the advent calendar?

He got **25 days.**

Life Observation Jokes

Which is faster, hot or cold?
Hot, because you can catch a cold.

Did you hear about the guy that ran into a window?
He was in a lot of pane.

What do you call a can opener that doesn't work?
A can't opener.

Why couldn't the skeleton cross the road?
He had no guts.

What did the ocean say to the sand?
Nothing, it just waved.

Ghosts are bad liars.
You can see right through them.

They arrested the devil. They charged him with possession.

I was going to tell a time travel joke, but you guys didn't like it.

Did you hear about the giant who threw up?
It's all over town.

I slept like a log last night.
I woke up in a fireplace.

My IQ results came back.
They were negative.

I hated facial hair
then it grew on me.

I stayed up all night wondering where the sun went.
Then it dawned on me.

How do you make holy water?
You boil the hell out of it.

Did you hear about the guy who has his left side cut off?
He's all right now.

What sound does a witch's car make?
Broom-broom.

What do you call a farmer who is really good at his job?
A man who is outstanding in his field.

Stop looking for the perfect match.
Use a lighter.

I gave away all my used batteries today, free of charge.

Which state has the most streets?

Rhode Island.

Did you hear about the claustrophobic astronaut?

They need a bit more space.

Why is it a bad idea to iron your four-leaf clover?

You shouldn't press your luck.

Want to hear a joke about construction?

I'm still working on it.

What did the fish say when it swam into a wall?

Dam.

What do you call a factory that sells passable products?
A satisfactory.

What rock group has four men that don't sing?
Mount Rushmore.

What's the name of a very polite French body of water?
Merci.

Why was the color green notoriously single?

Because it was so jaded.

What do you call a cute shortcoming?

A fl-aww.

Where's the best place to explore?

Rome.

What's the most useful type of hat?

A handy-cap.

How come Peter Pan keeps on flying?

Because he Neverlands.

My old best friend ran off years ago to pursue his dream of becoming a mime.

I haven't heard from him since.

What has a mouth
but no teeth?
A river.

It might take a village to raise a child... but it only takes a viking to raze a village.

What did the hat say to
the hat rack?
"You stay here, I'll go on ahead."

Why are skeletons so calm?
Because nothing gets under their skin.

How does the man on the moon cut his hair?
Eclipse it.

What did the DNA say to the other DNA?
"Do these genes make me look fat?"

Can February March?
No, but April May.

What do you call an
unpredictable camera?
A loose canon.

What genre are national
anthems?
Country.

How did the hacker escape the police?
He just ransomware!

How do celebrities stay cool?
They have many fans.

I recently took a pole. And found that 100% of the people in the tent were angry when it collapsed.

What is a pirate's favorite letter?
You would think it's 'R' but it's really the 'C'.

I have a fear of elevators, but I've started taking steps to avoid it.

Did you hear about the guy who invented the knock-knock joke?
He won the 'no-bell' prize.

A sandwich walks into a bar and the barman says, “sorry, we don’t serve food here.”

What did the young digital clock say to its Grandfather clock? **Look Grandpa, no hands!"**

Knock Knock / Who's there! / Shelby! / Shelby who? / Shelby comin' round the mountain when she comes!

Knock Knock / Who's there! / Dozen! / Dozen who? / Dozen anyone want to let me in!

A friend of mine didn't pay his exorcist.
He got repossessed.

I have a clean conscience.
It's never been used.

Knock Knock / Who's there! / Toodle! / Toodle who? / Bye, bye!

Knock Knock / Who's there! / Tank! / Tank who? / Your welcome!

Why did Humpty Dumpty have a great fall?

To make up for a lousy summer.

Why couldn't the psychic fit in the small shirt?

Because he was a medium.

What did the stone say to the hill?

Let's Rock and Roll.

Why did the scarecrow get an award?

Because he was outstanding in his field!

Purple is my favorite color!
I like it more than blue and red combined.

Does this bus stop at the river?

If it doesn't there'll be a very big splash.

What's the richest kind of air?

A millionaire.

What did one candle say to the other candle?
Are you going out tonight?

I wondered where my boomerang had gone.
Then it came back to me.

They really should call the Day After Tomorrow "Threemorrow".

How much will a pirate charge
you for a piercing?
Buck-an-ear.

What the sound of a
rainbow laughing?
Hue hue hue hue.

What did Death say when his
furniture was repossessed?
There will be reapercushions.

Healthy Jokes

What do you call a typo on a headstone?

A grave mistake.

What do you get the man who has everything?

Antibiotics.

My doctor told me I'm going deaf.

The news was hard for me to hear.

I told my doctor I heard buzzing. **SHe said it's a bug that's going around.**

Did I tell you why I can't become a doctor? **I don't have the patients.**

No one knew she had a dental implant until it came out in a conversation.

What did the pirate say on his 80th birthday?

Aye 'maighty.

Knock Knock / Who's there! / Flossie! / Flossie who? / Flossie your teeth everyday!

Knock Knock / Who's there! / Colin! / Colin who? / Colin the doctor, I feel ill!

Wanna hear a joke about Alzheimer's?
Never mind, I forgot.

Knock Knock / Who's there! / Dennis! / Dennis who? / Dennis says I need to have a tooth out!

Yesterday I accidentally swallowed some food coloring. The doctor says I’m okay but I feel like I’ve dyed a little inside.

The personal trainer at the gym advised me to try some resistance training. So far it's going really well. I've resisted going to the gym for six days now.

Food Jokes

Why don't eggs tell jokes?
They'd crack each other up.

What do you call mac and cheese that gets all up in your face?
Too close for comfort food.

Have you heard the joke about the butter?
I better not tell you, it might spread.

How do you fix a broken pizza?
Use tomato paste.

A cheese factory exploded
in France.
Da brie is everywhere.

I wrote a song about a tortilla.
It's a wrap.

I ate a clock the other day.
It was very time consuming.

Why did the strawberry cry?
His parents were in a jam.

What's all ears but
can't hear?
A cornfield.

Why did the orange lose the race?

It ran out of juice.

What does the nosey pepper do?

Get jalapeno business!

At one time I had the majority ownership shares in a top BBQ company. Somedays I wish I had never sold my stake.

How much room is needed for fungi to grow?

As mushroom as possible.

What did the pickle say to the cucumber?

Come on in the water's brine!

Why was the chef afraid of cooking steaks on a plane?

The steaks have never been higher.

How many apples grow on a tree?

All of them.

How do you make beef stew?

Tell a cow they're being watched.

What do you call a witch that goes to the beach?

A sandwich.

What do you call spaghetti that carries a fake ID?

an impasta!

What did the grape do when he got stepped on?

He let out a little wine.

My wife asked me the other day where I got so much candy. I said, "I always have a few Twix up my sleeve."

I burned 2000 calories today, I left my food in the oven for too long.

Waitress: How did you find your steak sir?
Me: I just looked next to the potatoes and there it was.

I could tell a joke about pizza, but it's a little cheesy.

Why do the French eat snails?
They don't like fast food.

I ordered a chicken and an egg from Amazon. I'll let you know what comes first.

What did the daddy tomato say to the baby tomato?
A: catch up!

Knock Knock / Who's there? / Cheese! / Cheese who? / Cheese a jolly good fellow!

Knock Knock / Who's there? / Curry! / Curry who? / Curry me back home will you!

Knock Knock / Who's there! / Beets! / Beets who? / Beets me, but I just forgot the joke!

Knock Knock / Who's there! / Four Eggs! / Four Eggs who? / Four Eggs ample!

What do you call bread's ability to smell?

Naan sense!

What happens to garlic sauce over time?

The sausages.

Gaining Weight?
...It's a piece of cake!

What do you call an
immature carrot?
A baby carrot.

Why does the corn
hate the farmer?
**Because he picks his
ears!**

What's cold, hot and chilly all at once?
Cold chili.

Want to hear a cheesy joke?
I will only tell you if I have your Parmesan.

What did Buddha say to the Pizza guy?
"Make me one with everything."

Did you hear about the pessimistic German vegetarian?

He feared the wurst.

What's a calendar's favorite fruit?

Dates.

Why are sandwiches better in space?
They are always a bit meteor.

Why did the little refrigerator salute the big refrigerator?
Because he was General Electric.

Animal and Pet Jokes

Dogs can't operate MRI machines but catscan.

What breed of dog can jump higher than a skyscraper?
Any breed. Skyscrapers can't jump.

What do you call a sleeping bull?
A bulldozer.

What did the evill chicken lay?
Deviled eggs.

Why did the man name his dog Rolex?
Because it was a watchdog.

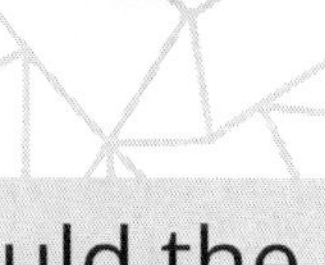

How could the dolphin afford to buy a house ?
He prawned everything!

What kind of car does a sheep drive?
A lamborghini.

Why can't the leopard hide?
He's always spotted.

WHat do most cows like to read?
Cattle-logs.

What's a cow's favorite moosical note?

Beef-flat!

Why don't oysters give to charity?

Because they're shellfish.

What do cats major in college?

String theory!

What do you get when you cross a duck and a firework?

A firequacker.

What do they feed a gorilla when he goes to Paris?

Ape Suzettes!

What do you call eight rabbits walking backwards together?

A receding hare-line.

How did the cowboy know his pony was getting sick?
He was a little hoarse.

Where do Polar Bears keep their money?
In the Snowbank.

What do you call a horse who likes to carry all the groceries?
A one trip pony.

How can a dog afford
to go to college?
Furnancial Aid.

Why was the father
centipede annoyed?
**Because all of his children
needed new shoes.**

What did father bee say
to his rebelling son?
Beehive!

What is the clumsiest bee?
A bumbling bee.

What do you call a fish in orbit?
Trouterspace.

What did father buffalo say to child buffalo as he left for school?
Bison.

Knock Knock / Who's there! / P! / P who? / P Nuts are an elephants favorite treat!

Knock Knock / Who's there! / Catskills! / Catskills who? / Catskills mice!

How do you communicate with the Loch Ness Monster at 20000 fathoms?

Drop him a line.

Why isn't there gambling at the zoo?
Too many cheetahs.

Why don't seagulls fly over the bay?
Because then they'd be bay-gulls!

What kind of dog did the sad cantaloupe get?
A melon collie!

How did the farmer find his lost cow?

He tractor down.

How do you fix a broken gorilla?

With a monkey wrench.

Why did the cowboy buy a dachshund?

He wanted to get a long little doggy.

How can you tell elephants love to travel ?
They are always packing their trunks!

I can't take my dog to the pond because the ducks keep attacking him.
That's what I get for buying a pure-bread dog.

Sports Jokes

What do sprinters eat before the race?
Nothing, they fast!

Why do Dads take an extra pair of socks when they go golfing?
In case they get a hole in one.

Why did the coach go to the bank?
To get his quarter back.

I wondered why the baseball was getting bigger.
Then it hit me.

What's the difference between a poorly dressed man on a tricycle and a well-dressed man on a bicycle?
Attire.

Why did the gym close down?
It didn't work out.

Why couldn't the bicycle stand up?

Because it was two tired.

Why don't NFL players wear glasses?

Because it's a contact sport.

Why should you never date a tennis player?

Because love means nothing to them.

Hobby Jokes

I'm trying to organize a hide-and-seek tournament.
But good players are really hard to find.

What kind of car does a ghost drive?
A boogati!

Two giant windmills are out on a hilltop. One turns to the other and asks, "What kind of music do you like?"
The other one says, "I'm a really big metal fan."

What is an autobiography?
The story of an automobile.

Luke Skywalker is well on his way to completing his comic book collection... ...he's already got all the daddy issues.

Knock Knock / Who's there! / Cartoon! / Cartoon who? / Cartoon up just fine, she purrs like a cat!

Knock Knock / Who's there! / Yah! / Yah who? / Ride em cowboy!

Did you hear about the big Lego sale?
People were lined up for blocks.

I just finished making a belt out of watches. It was a waist of time.

I am writing a book about the history of camping. It's all in past tents.

What monsters are all the tools in the toolbox afraid of?
Vampliers.

Why do guitar amps hum?
Because they don't know the words.

Tech Jokes

Dad, my laptop's frozen. Have you tried warming it up?

I can never talk to my Dad at breakfast because he still reads newspapers. I guess you could say he's behind The Times.

What does a baby computer call it's father? **Data.**

What time of day are you not able to find your watch?

4:04.

What does a computer say when it encounters a skunk?

C PU.

Work Jokes

I got fired from the keyboard factory today... It seems I wasn't putting enough shifts.

To whoever stole my copy of Microsoft Office, I will find you. You have my Word.

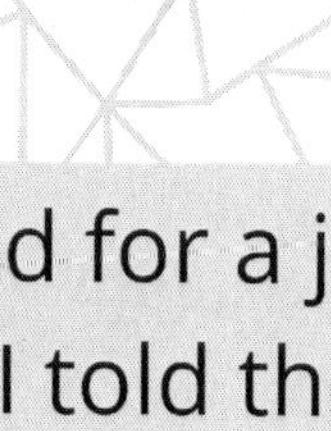

I just applied for a job down at the diner. I told them I really bring a lot to the table.

They're building a mirror factory in my town. I could see myself working there.

My dad got fired from the local calendar shop. He kept taking days off.

My Dad told me "always fight fire with fire"... And that's why he's no longer a fireman.

My boss told me to have a good day, so I went home.

What do you call a priest who quits to become a lawyer?
A father in law.

Knock Knock / Who's there! / Bean! / Bean who? / Bean working very hard today!

Why can't truck drivers ever fully retire? Because they can only semi retire.

Did you hear about the Chicken who went for his job interview? **He got roasted!**

If loving copies is wrong, I don't want to be copyright.

Why did the invisible man turn down the job offer?

He couldn't see himself doing it.

What did the accountant say while auditing a document?

This is taxing.

Did you hear about the girl who quit working at the donut factory?

She was fed up with the whole business.

Why couldn't the post-it note make it to his son's birthday party?

Because he was stuck at the office!

Manufactured by Amazon.ca
Acheson, AB

14587028R00057